Richie's Rocket

BY JOAN ANDERSON

PHOTOGRAPHED BY GEORGE ANCONA

RICHIE

HAMPTON-BROWN BOOKS
MANY CULTURES, MANY LANGUAGES...MANY POSSIBILITIES!™

ACKNOWLEDGMENTS

We'd like to thank Luka Tacon and his mom for providing the talent for this book. Students in Janice Abbott's class at I.S. 174 School in Bronx, New York, were responsible for the design, building, and delivery of Richie's rocketship. Joan Daniel helped scout talent and location. The Air and Space Museum and NASA provided research materials and some photographs. Without all your help, *Richie's Rocket* could never have blasted off!

Joan Anderson
George Ancona

Photo insets pp. 11, 13, 19, 21, 29 courtesy of the National Aeronautics and Space Administration.

Text copyright © 1993 by Joan Anderson.
Illustrations copyright © 1993 by George Ancona.
Reprinted by permission of Morrow Junior Books, a division of William Morrow & Company, Inc.

Hampton-Brown Books
P.O. Box 223220
Carmel, California 93922
(800) 333-3510

Printed in the United States of America.

ISBN 1-56334-736-9

02 03 04 10

To Janice Abbott for her creative impulse and friendship
—J. A.

To Cousin Richie and Iris
—G. A.

Something was up. Richie Rodriguez's mother was sure of it. Ever since she had taken him to the planetarium, Richie had practically been living on the roof of their apartment building. He came down only to eat or take something from his room or borrow one of his father's tools. Then he was out the door again.

After a few days of this, Richie's mother got curious and climbed the six flights of stairs to the roof. She wanted to see what he was up to.

As she pushed open the heavy metal door, her eyes grew wide with amazement. There, in the middle of the roof, sat a giant something.

"Boo!" shouted Richie, popping out from behind the huge box. "You're standing on my launchpad. What do you think of my spaceship?"

Richie's mother gasped. "So this is what you've been doing." When she peered inside and saw the complicated control panel, she shook her head in wonder. "You sure have thought of everything," she said. "Now, don't fly off without telling me. I wouldn't want to miss the blast-off!"

One hot summer evening, Richie was on the roof, staring at the sky through one of his rocket's windows. He had never been up there so late. Moonlight bounced off the silver-colored rocket, making it positively glisten.

Leaning back in his seat, Richie searched for the Big Dipper. "There it is," he whispered, grabbing on to the steering wheel and pretending to pilot his rocket through the stars. He turned each and every switch to the on position, just in case Mission Control ordered a launch.

"Five, four, three, two, one," he recited, leaning back and closing his sleepy eyes. "Ignition! We have ignition."

And then there was a noise like an explosion. Everything was shaking! Holding tight to the arms of his seat, Richie saw orange smoke everywhere. *Crackle, crackle, crunch, crackle.* The little rocket trembled and shook. There was another loud boom, and suddenly he was moving…up, UP, UP! Richie felt as if a giant rock was pushing him into the back of his seat. It was scary. He squeezed his eyes shut and held his breath.

As the rocket picked up speed, it lurched one way and whirled another, spinning so fast that Richie's stomach did flip-flops. "Yuck!" he said. "I feel really dizzy. Maybe I don't want to be an astronaut after all." But it was too late to turn back. His rocket thrust upward, past the clouds and into space!

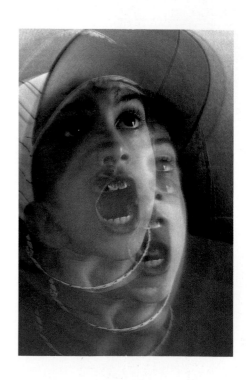

Almost as fast as all the rumbling had begun, it stopped. Now there was silence... eerie silence. The engines had shut off, and Richie's rocket coasted through a soundless sky, looking almost like a runaway balloon.

"Now what do I do?" Richie wondered.

"Where am I?" he said aloud, peering out the ceiling window. He saw only nothingness that stretched out forever. It felt kind of lonely. Then he caught sight of something far, far away that looked like a beach ball.

"Wow!" Richie gasped. "That's Earth floating beneath me. I'm up higher than I thought."

Curious to see more, Richie reached for his seat belt and unhitched it. When he did, he drifted straight out of his seat and floated right up to the ceiling.

"Whoa!" Richie said as he bumped into the control panel. "Wait a minute." He reached for his seat to steady himself but found that his arms didn't seem to work. It felt as if he was underwater. Remembering some swimming strokes, he began to move around, using his arms for balance. "Whee, this is fun," Richie exclaimed as he began tumbling from one spot to another. "This is easier than moving around on Earth."

It didn't take Richie long to adjust to being in space. And once he felt comfortable, he was eager to settle down and enjoy the ride.

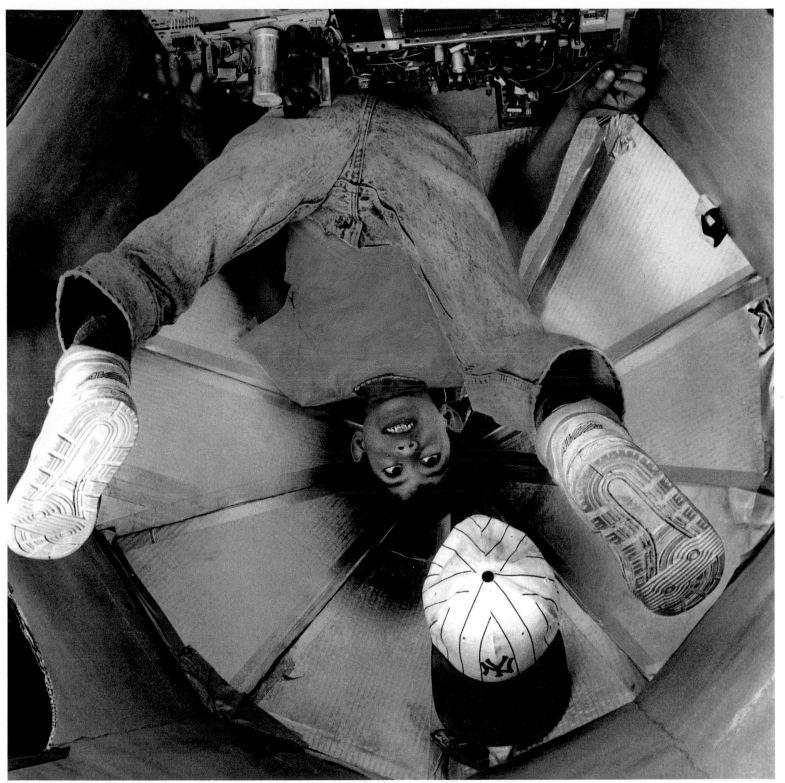

He snuggled back down into his seat and fastened himself in. "Now for a snack," Richie said, pleased that he'd brought his lunch box along.

No sooner did he raise the lid than an apple floated right up into the cabin. So did a giant chocolate-chip cookie, his notebook, and everything else that had been packed away. Richie tried to reach out and grab his stuff, but he couldn't get a grip on anything.

"Weightlessness," he said, shaking his head in frustration and hoping one of his snacks would eventually drift back into reach.

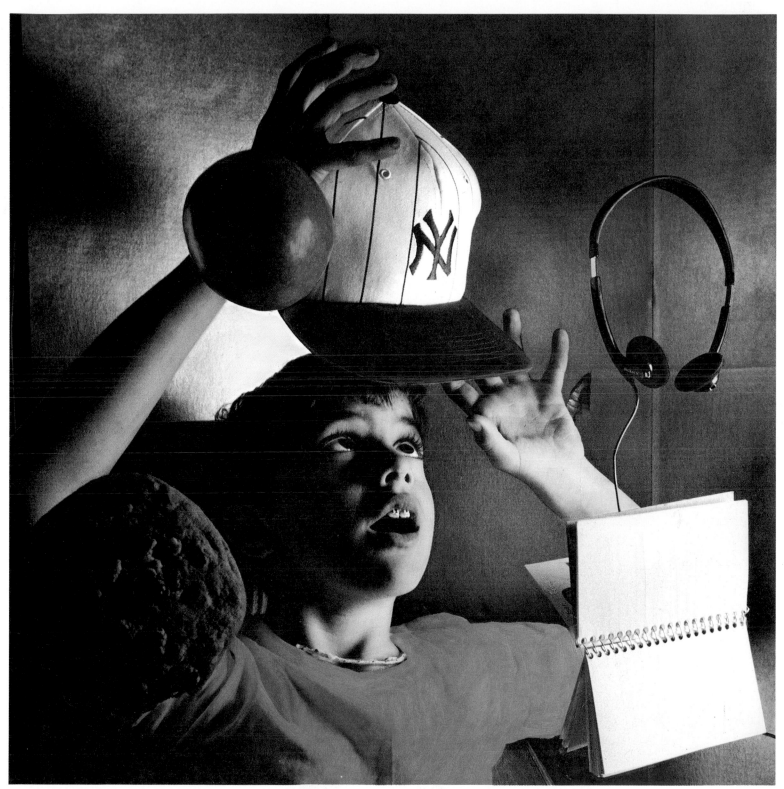

Just then there was a knock on the window, and a face appeared. "Yipes," Richie yelped, half scared out of his wits. "Who are you?"

"Hi," said the other astronaut. "I'm from the spacecraft straight ahead. We saw your rocket ship, and my crew sent me over to inspect you."

Richie felt proud that his rocket looked so real. "Where are you headed?" he asked.

"The moon," the astronaut answered. "Want to come along?"

Richie didn't have to stop and think. He just said yes.

"Good. We'll tow you along."

Richie could feel his rocket being drawn toward the spaceship like a magnet. For the first time during his flight he felt as though he could sit back and enjoy the scenery. Above him, far off in the dark sky, was what looked like a fireworks display. "Are they comets?" Richie wondered, gazing at their long fiery tails.

Soon Richie saw a warm glow, and he leaned forward to see what was shining. The moon! There it was, looking all craggy and dimpled and very, very bright.

Suddenly a voice in his earphones said, "Spacecraft to rocket. Prepare to deploy your landing gear." Richie pushed his landing button, hoping it would work.

"We're dropping you off," the voice from the other ship said. "Pick you up after our next orbit." And then Richie and his rocket began tumbling downward.

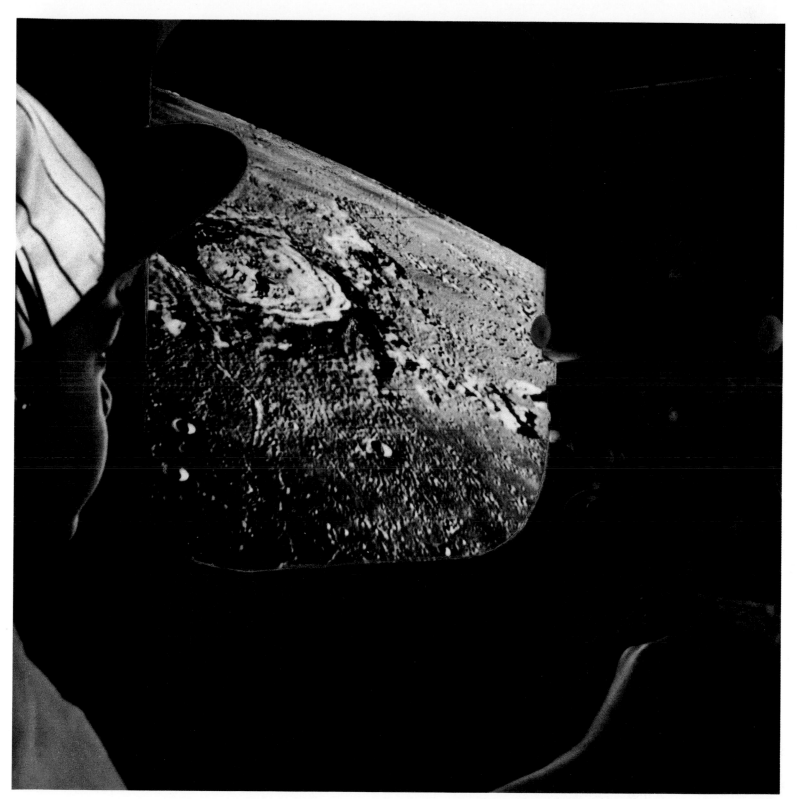

"Well, here I go," Richie said, his heart pounding. He swallowed hard. It was as if he was taking a slow elevator ride. The huge moon loomed all around him. And then, seconds later, he felt a thump and then...*splat!*

"Touchdown!" Richie yelped. At least he thought it was, but with all the moon dust floating around, he couldn't see a thing.

Gradually he began to make out a great silvery landscape with giant boulders and grayish mounds.

"I'm outta here," Richie announced, unbuckling his seat belt and throwing open the hatch. "Hello, moon," he hollered. "Anyone home?"

And with that, Richie jumped down. But as soon as his toes touched the surface, he bounced right back up to his rocket! "Hey, what's going on?" he asked. Then Richie remembered. Walking on the moon is like moving across a trampoline. You have to tiptoe gently or you'll be jumping like a kangaroo.

It took a few minutes getting used to his moon legs. But gradually Richie discovered that he could get around by moving as if he were jumping rope. He hopped and bounced and somersaulted from one mound to another—and in one big leap landed on top of a peak.

"Wow!" he said, leaping from peak to peak.

He tried to skim stones, like he did at the beach back home, but they just drifted off and away.

Then Richie had an idea. "I'll write my name in the moon dust. That way everyone will know I was here!" And he did.

Just then, he spotted the spacecraft and quickly hopped back to his own little rocket.

"Hey! Here I am!" Richie screamed, jumping up and down and waving his arms, hoping the astronauts would notice. With no one to talk to or play with, the spaceship was a welcome sign of life.

Richie eagerly climbed aboard his rocket. He couldn't wait to hook up with the spaceship again. He fastened himself into his seat, switched on the engine, and waited for instructions.

"Spacecraft to rocket. Spacecraft to rocket. Ready for departure?"

"I sure am," Richie sighed.

"We have a message from Mission Control," the voice from the other craft continued. "They want you back on Earth."

"All right by me," Richie said, relieved to be going home.

Soon the elevator ride began, pulling his rocket toward the spaceship. Then Richie felt a huge push, and the next thing he knew, he was soaring through space.

"Phew!" he said, leaning toward the window and gazing at the beautiful planet getting bigger and bigger beneath him.

When Richie heard thunder, he knew that his engine had started and he was safely in Earth's atmosphere. He saw the city, and minutes later he was in a blur of clouds.

He closed his eyes and waited, hoping for a perfect landing, and suddenly…*plop!* Opening his eyes, Richie saw the familiar smokestack on the apartment roof and the friendly sight of clothes hanging up to dry. "Mission accomplished," Richie announced as he opened the hatch and climbed out.

Richie took a deep whiff of the early-morning air. "Hello, Earth," he said, looking down at all the activity on the street below. Then he looked back at his little rocket.

Richie's stomach growled just as he heard his mother's voice calling to him from the kitchen window below. "Richie...time for breakfast."

He bounded down the stairwell. For once, Richie was ready to spend some time at home.